Taking a Stand

Being a Leader & Helping Others

ABDO
Publishing Company

Strong, Beautiful Girls

Taking a Stand

Being a Leader & Helping Others

by MK Ehrman

Content Consultant
Vicki F. Panaccione, PhD
Licensed Child Psychologist
Founder, Better Parenting Institute

Credits

Published by ABDO Publishing Company, 8000 West 78th Street, Edina, Minnesota 55439. Copyright © 2009 by Abdo Consulting Group, Inc. International copyrights reserved in all countries. No part of this book may be reproduced in any form without written permission from the publisher. The Essential Library™ is a trademark and logo of ABDO Publishing Company.

Printed in the United States of America, North Mankato, Minnesota.
012009
062011
Special thanks to Dr. Vicki Panaccione for her expertise and guidance in shaping this series.

Editors: Amy Van Zee, Holly Saari
Copy Editor: Erika Wittekind
Interior Design and Production: Becky Daum
Cover Design: Becky Daum

Library of Congress Cataloging-in-Publication Data
Ehrman, MK
 Taking a stand : being a leader & helping others / by MK Ehrman.
   p. cm. — (Essential health : strong, beautiful girls)
 Includes index.
 ISBN 978-1-60453-105-3
 1. Girls—Life skills guides. 2. Attitude (Psychology) 3. Girls—Conduct of life. I. Title.

 HQ777.E74 2009
 646.700835'2—dc22

                         2008015211

Contents

Meet Dr. Vicki

Throughout the series Strong, Beautiful Girls, you'll hear the reassuring, knowledgeable voice of Dr. Vicki Panaccione, a licensed psychologist with more than 25 years of experience working with teens, children, and families. Dr. Vicki offers her expert advice to girls who find themselves in the difficult situations described in each chapter.

Better known as the Parenting Professor™, Dr. Vicki is founder of the Better Parenting Institute™ and author of *Discover Your Child* and *What Your Kids Would Tell You . . . If Only You'd Ask!* You might have seen her name quoted in publications such as the *New York Times*, *Family Circle*, and *Parents* magazine.

While her credentials run deep, perhaps what qualifies her most to advise girls on everything from body image to friendship to schoolwork is that she's been there, so she can relate. "I started out in junior high as the chubby new kid with glasses and freckles, who the popular kids loved to tease or even worse . . . ignore," says the doc. "They should see me now!"

Today, Dr. Vicki maintains a private practice in Melbourne, Florida, and writes articles for a variety of periodicals and Web sites. She has been interviewed or quoted in major publications including *Parenting* magazine, *Reader's Digest*, *First for Women*, and *Woman's World*, networks such as Fox, ABC, NBC, and CBS, and several popular Web sites. Dr. Vicki joined esteemed colleagues Tony Robbins, Dr. Wayne Dyer, and Bill Bartmann as coauthor of *The Power of Team*, the latest in the best-selling series Wake Up and Live the Life You Love. She is an adviser for the Web site parentalwisdom.com and also for MTV/Nickelodeon's parentsconnect.com. She is a clinical consultant for Red Line Editorial, Inc. Not to mention, she's the proud mother of Alex, her 21-year-old son who is pursuing his PhD to become a medical researcher.

With all that she has going for her now, it might be hard to imagine that Dr. Vicki was ever an awkward teen struggling to find her way. But consider this—she's living proof that no matter how bleak things might look now, they do get better. The following stories and Dr. Vicki's guidance will help you discover your own path to happiness and success, becoming the Strong, Beautiful Girl you are meant to be.

Take It from Me

I'm going to begin with a little confession: I am hardly what you'd call a natural-born leader. When I was going through those awkward pre-teen and early-teen years, I was shy and lacked self-confidence (something the pretty and popular kids at school didn't seem to struggle with). I never imagined I could succeed at anything. What can I say? I was one of the geeks.

So what am I doing writing this book about success and leadership? Well, that's where the good news comes in. I have since learned that natural gifts and abilities only get you so far. The real keys to success and leadership are effort and attitude.

It might surprise you to learn that many of the successful adults I've spoken with went through the same self-doubt you might be experiencing. They tell me that when they were young, they never imagined that they would get as far as they have. Like I did, they felt that others were more popular, skilled, talented, and just plain smarter than they were. Does that sound familiar to you? What we all had in common was that we were willing to change, and that's really all you need to get started on the road to leadership and success. Is it going to be easy? Well, nothing worthwhile in life is easy. You have to be willing to put yourself out in the world, take a few risks, and most importantly, you need to see yourself as someone who can lead people and bring home the blue ribbon.

Obviously, this book can't cover all of the challenges and disappointments you may face as you work toward success throughout your life, nor can it list every single issue you will face when trying to lead others. But what I do hope is that by showing you how other girls have struggled with the very same issues, you will see that perhaps your case is not as different as you might have imagined. If I can do that, then my efforts at leadership will have been a success, something I never would have imagined when I was your age. And, if you're ready to make a few adjustments in your own mental outlook, the same successes can be yours.

XOXO,
MK

1

The
Loser

It's the nature of competition. Somebody wins, and the rest, well . . . don't. If every runner came in first in every race, if all the candidates won every election, if every piece of art took home the blue ribbon, there wouldn't be much point to the contest, would there? Competition is good because the desire to win makes us dig a little deeper and try a little harder so we can find out what we're truly capable of accomplishing. But it's hard to come up short—in fact, it just plain hurts. And for those who live in the shadow of an older, more successful sibling, these feelings can be twice as bad and last twice as long. Suddenly, we switch from "I didn't win this time" to "I knew I shouldn't have tried. I never win anything." You feel like there's a big "L" on your forehead, and that everyone around you thinks you're a loser.

Thinking this way can hold you back even more than tying your shoelaces together before the start of a race. The only trouble is that it's very difficult to get rid of these thoughts once they become set in your mind. To do that, you need to enter a different kind of contest—one that takes place entirely inside your own head!

The contest begins by cutting yourself a break. Giving yourself permission not to be the best and still feel good about yourself is the first step on the path to victory. The contest continues as you realize that not being successful in one area just means that you haven't found the area that's right for you yet. If you think you aren't good at anything, you need to take a look at your strengths and weaknesses to figure out where you can shine.

If you think you aren't good at anything, you need to take a look at your strengths and weaknesses to figure out where you can shine.

Ming felt like a failure compared to her super successful older sister. Read on to find out how she coped with feeling as if she never quite measured up.

Ming's Story

Growing up, Ming always felt it was a curse to follow behind an older sister such as Kim. Kim seemed to succeed so effortlessly at everything she tried, while Ming felt like a failure in comparison. Ming was a decent student. She got plenty of As and never any Cs, but compared to the perfect report cards that Kim brought home, she felt very average. Kim was cheerleader of the year in junior high, and Ming didn't even make the squad. Kim was captain of the girl's volleyball team and had taken the school to the regional championships.

Ming wanted to play volleyball too, and tried out for the team. Tryouts didn't go so well for her, though, and afterward the coach gently told Ming that she didn't have what it took to play on the team.

"I guess some people are just doomed to fail," she told herself as she sat in the locker room. "Why did I even think I could do it?" When she heard the rest of the girls giggling as they returned from the volleyball court, she grabbed her things and ran out before any of them could see her.

Talk About It

- Why did Ming run out of the locker room and not stay to talk to the other girls?

- Have you ever failed at something you really wanted to succeed at? How did you feel? How did you deal with it?

When Ming got home, she saw a trophy on the table—Kim's. "Look, honey," her mother said. "Your sister got first place at the cheerleading competition. Isn't that great?"

Ming felt her face get very hot. She felt angry and embarrassed at the same time. Everyone was waiting for her to say something, but she couldn't speak.

"Everything go okay at volleyball tryouts?" her father asked gently.

"Oh, who cares?" Ming cried, running up the stairs to her room. "I don't know why I even tried out for the team. Everybody knows I suck at volleyball. I suck at everything!"

Talk About It

- Why didn't Ming want to face her family? Have you ever felt that way? Why?

- Would Ming have preferred that no one asked her about volleyball? Why?

- Is there a better way Ming could have handled the situation? What advice would you give her?

Alone in her room, Ming threw herself on her bed. She wasn't good enough at volleyball to make the team and couldn't do any of the other things her sister was so good at. In a few minutes, her mother came in and sat down next to her. "Ming, you shouldn't say things like that," her mother told her. "Everybody is good at something."

"But every time I try to do something, I always fail," Ming answered through her tears. "I feel like I'm the biggest loser."

"But every time I try to do something, I always fail," Ming answered through her tears. "I feel like I'm the biggest loser."

"Maybe you spend so much time trying to be Kim that you forget how to be Ming," her mother answered.

Talk About It

- **What does Ming's mother mean when she says Ming is trying to be Kim and not herself?**
- **Have you ever tried to be like somebody you looked up to? How did that work out?**
- **Do you think Ming's mother is giving her good advice? Why?**

Ming thought about what her mother said. She had been focusing so much on following in her sister's footsteps that she hadn't really been looking for her own path. She was bound to be good at something, and she was determined to figure it out.

Later, when Ming came back downstairs, she saw that her father was ready to go out, while everyone else was sitting in the living room.

"Ming," her sister told her, "Dad's going out for ice cream to help us celebrate. But you know, it would be even better if we had some of your chocolate chunk brownies to go with it."

"Oh, that's right, Ming," her mother chimed in. "No one makes brownies better than you. You are the best baker in this family, not to mention the best cook in the house."

Later, as Ming mixed the chocolate chunks, cocoa, flour, eggs, and sugar, she found herself feeling much better. She knew her family was just trying to cheer her up, and she appreciated that they cared. It was true—she could make some pretty awesome brownies! And who knows, maybe she'd start whipping up other things in the kitchen for her family—she definitely did know how to make some scrumptious dishes.

Talk About It

- Why does baking brownies make Ming feel better? In what way does this help Ming change her attitude?

- What are some talents you have? How are you using them?

- What are some of the things you do well because you worked on improving yourself? How did you do it?

Ming's mother was right. Ming was so busy trying to be Kim that she didn't pay attention to who she was. She set up a competition in her head that didn't really exist. No one else thought she was a loser. She just wasn't Kim.

When you start thinking about yourself in terms of who you are (such as saying to yourself, "I'm a loser") rather than what you did ("my skills weren't strong enough for the team"), you set up a negative view of yourself and stop believing in your own abilities.

Was it okay that Ming wasn't great at volleyball? Sure. Not everyone has that talent. All you can do is your personal best and discover your own special talents like Ming did.

Get Healthy

1. Pay attention to the way you talk to yourself. Instead of calling yourself a loser or stupid, make a list of your strong points as well as areas you think you need to improve. And remember, just because you may not succeed at one thing does not mean that you can't succeed at anything!

2. If you're not sure what you're good at, try several different activities. You might try sports teams, music groups, arts and crafts, or other hobbies. If something isn't

a perfect fit for you, don't be afraid to try something else!

3. It's good to challenge yourself, but start with something easy. Once you realize you can accomplish something, make your challenges a little more difficult. That's how you develop a winner's attitude.

4. Reward yourself! Give yourself a little treat when you make progress, like the shoes you always wanted or maybe your favorite cookie from the bakery. If you don't succeed, don't punish yourself. Just learn from your mistakes. Set another goal, perhaps taking smaller steps, and try again.

The Last Word from MK

These days, girls are expected to compete and succeed at nearly everything. This can be confusing at first, especially when you keep finding yourself outside of the "winner's circle." Many girls begin to think that something is wrong with them instead of just realizing that they weren't the best in that particular activity on that particular day. The trick is to avoid comparing yourself with others and to start thinking about what you're good at and where you'd like to improve. Once you begin looking at things that way, then no matter what happens, you can't lose!

2

The Quitter

Having the proper attitude is important. But is that all it takes to succeed? Of course not! You'll find that the road to success has many detours. No doubt you'll come across obstacles that can lead you away from your goal. Often, when the excitement about a new project passes and the work becomes a little frustrating, you begin to doubt yourself and think that maybe your great idea wasn't so great after all. It suddenly becomes so tempting to drop what you're doing and start something new so you can get that excited "just-started" feeling all over again. But of course, not finishing is one way to guarantee that you won't succeed.

Sometimes, if you're lucky, you get that one special person who comes along and encourages you by saying, "Keep it up. It's going to be great!" Other times, you have to be that person for yourself. But here's the good news: You don't have to be extra smart, extra fast, or extra talented to keep yourself motivated. You only have to set your mind to do everything you can to reach your goal. And before you know it, you'll be feeling that great rush of having turned an idea in your head into something real that other people can see, read, watch, or even taste.

Megan wanted to try everything, but she lost interest before reaching any of her goals. It ended up taking an extra push for her to follow through on one of her many projects.

Megan's Story

Megan was a girl with lots of ideas, and most of them sounded like good ones. You couldn't say for certain, though, because while Megan would begin some new project full of excitement and energy, somehow she'd just never get

Megan wanted to try everything, but she lost interest before reaching any of her goals.

around to finishing it. She had signed up to compete in the big race at school. But after a few days of trying to improve her running speed, she stopped practicing altogether. "Rose is the fastest girl in the school anyway," she figured. "So why bother?"

Megan was hoping to win first place at the science fair. She told her teacher, Ms. Hingle, that her project was going to be on how different colored lights affect the growth of tomato plants. Ms. Hingle thought it was a great idea, and Megan was excited. When she set up the lamps and put in the colored bulbs, it seemed like she was making her own pretty rainbow right in her basement. But then she got to the part where she had to measure the growth of the plants and record the numbers. She started getting bored. "Does anybody really care about what colored light does to plants?" Megan thought. "What if people find out about this and start teasing me?" She started believing it was a stupid idea and that she really didn't care about dumb old tomatoes, anyway. So instead of continuing, she texted her friend Laura to see if she wanted to hang out.

Talk About It

- Why did Megan lose interest in her plants?

- Should Megan have stayed home to work on her project instead of hanging out with Laura? Why?

- Have you ever had to choose between doing something fun and finishing something important? What did you do?

The fair came and Megan hadn't finished her project. Still, she felt that none of the other projects were as good as what she had planned to do. She stopped at the project that had won first place. "Measuring how fast ice melts at different temperatures," she said in a snotty tone. "Who hasn't seen that before? Mine would have been much, much better."

Louisa overheard Megan talking about her project.

"Well, if your idea was so great," she challenged Megan, "where is your project?"

Megan tried to say something clever back to Louisa, but nothing came to her lips.

Talk About It

- **Why do you think Megan acted rudely when talking about Louisa's project? What do you think Megan was actually annoyed about?**

- **Have you ever watched somebody win a prize when you thought you could have done better? How did you feel?**

"I know my project could have won first place," Megan said to Ms. Hingle. "It's not fair!"

"I'm sure it could have, Megan," Ms. Hingle replied gently. "But in this world, we're judged on what we actually do, not on what we say we're going to do. Not only did you get an incomplete, which brings your grade down, but it sounds like your idea may have had a chance to win first place and go to the district competition."

"I kept meaning to finish," Megan said. "But I started getting so unsure of myself. Maybe I'll write a funny essay about it for the essay contest."

"Megan, it's great to think of new ideas, but first you've got to finish what you have already started," Ms. Hingle said. "Sometimes you have to stop thinking about what might go wrong and just keep going. If you leave things unfinished, how do you ever expect to win first place or get a good grade? I can't give a passing grade to an incomplete assignment. And judges can't judge a project that isn't there. Why don't you finish your science project and bring it to me in two weeks?"

"Megan, it's great to think of new ideas, but first you've got to finish what you have already started," Ms. Hingle said.

Talk About It

- Why would it be a bad idea for Megan to start writing an essay?

- Why do you think Ms. Hingle wanted Megan to finish her science project? Was it to help her grade or was there another reason?

- What will Megan learn by finishing her original project?

Megan went home and set up the colored lights again. She got some new little tomato plants and potted them in the soil. After a week, she got tired of measuring the plants, and writing the results on the graph seemed like too much work. She wanted to make an ice-cream sundae or watch a movie. Instead, she took a deep breath and told herself, "I just have to finish this one part today and then I can make that sundae—with extra whipped cream!" When she finished her work and finally did make that sundae, it seemed like the best one she had ever tasted.

Talk About It

- Have you ever wished you had followed through with something? What did you do?

- Do you have any unfinished projects or assignments right now? What could you do about them?

Ask Dr. Vicki

Getting the job done is one of the toughest lessons to learn about success. When the excitement of a new idea has passed and the self-doubts began to creep in, Megan had to learn to push discouragement aside to continue toward her goal. Until she gets more experience, Megan won't realize that having doubts, frustrations, and fears is completely normal. If all inventors stopped what they were doing because of boredom or self-doubt, we still would be reading by candlelight and riding horses instead of cars!

Before you start thinking about the big prize, you need to know what it's like to create something that wouldn't be there if you hadn't completed it. Coming up with good ideas and having good intentions are important first steps to reaching a goal. But the trick is to make finishing the most important goal. When you've done that, you will win the contest against your inner fears and develop the determination to stick with it even when you have doubts or something more fun to do. You also will find that the more you complete, the more confidence you will have in your ability to finish the next project. And that's a more valuable prize than even the biggest trophy.

Get Healthy

1. Set yourself a realistic goal, something you know you can complete. Break down the task into steps or stages, and decide how much time you need to spend on each. Then, make a schedule and stick to it. By the time it is due, you will have finished the job.

2. Once you've decided that your idea is worth doing, go into the "no judgment" zone. That means no judging it, fearing it, or delaying it. Then, just keep your eye on the prize.

3. If you need to, set up little rewards for yourself every time you finish a step. For example, you can have ice cream or watch a movie, but only after the whole step has been completed!

The Last Word from MK

If you are like Megan and tend to quit before finishing, then the lessons she learned can be really helpful to you. The sooner in life you learn to be a Finisher and not a Quitter, the sooner you can move forward on the road to success. By finishing what you start you will learn that through your determination you can actually turn ideas into real accomplishments. After all, no one's ever won a race by quitting along the way. Crossing the finish line is the only possible way to win!

3

The Blur

While some people want nothing more than a taste of success, no matter how small, others have the opposite problem. They have all the qualities needed to successfully achieve their goals. They have a positive attitude, they are focused and determined, and they know how to apply themselves. What they don't know how to do is enjoy their successes once they are achieved.

Even more importantly, girls often forget that no accomplishment can replace a healthy diet, proper sleep, and the precious bonds they make with family and friends. Of course, part of the determination to succeed is the willingness to sacrifice a few hours of sleep or miss a family outing from time to time. But like so much in life, this is all a matter of balance. When determination and focus turn into obsession, everything else starts to fall apart.

For some people, it takes a shock to the system—an illness, perhaps—to make them realize that they are pushing themselves too far and need to slow down and enjoy life a little more. But this doesn't have to happen to you.

When determination and focus turn into obsession, everything else starts to fall apart.

The trick is learning to recognize the warning signs and take action before it's too late.

Take Zoe, for example. She learned the hard way that trying to do too much can have unexpected consequences.

Zoe's Story

Zoe never stopped. She was captain of the girl's basketball team and played first chair violin in the school orchestra. She studied hard and always got As. When the student honor roll went out, her name was always on it. She started a mentor's club to help tutor younger children who were behind in their classes. The mayor of her town even sent her a letter of thanks. With so much going for her, it seemed like Zoe would be the happiest girl in school. But she never slowed down long enough to enjoy her successes. Her classmates even nicknamed her "The Blur."

At lunchtime, Zoe barely touched her food before running off to the library to work on an extra-credit book report. After school, she headed right to basketball practice. When she got home, she would pull out her violin and start to practice. At night, she turned off the lights in her room but stayed up in the dark typing reports on her computer.

Her teachers and coaches had nothing but praise for Zoe. But at home, things were different. Her parents worked very hard, too, and they seemed to take Zoe's accomplishments for granted. When she proudly showed the mayor's letter to her father, he just replied, "Of course, dear. We expect nothing less." Zoe shrugged, put the letter in a drawer, and decided she would learn a violin solo and audition for the school talent contest.

Talk About It

- Why do you think Zoe works as hard as she does?

- What did Zoe expect her parents to say about the mayor's letter? How did she feel about her father's reaction?

- Have you ever done something you were very proud of only to have nobody notice? How did you feel?

One day, Zoe overheard some girls talking about a birthday party they had gone to over the weekend. It was for Melissa, whom Zoe considered one of her close friends, but she hadn't even been invited. Zoe suddenly realized that she hadn't been invited to anything for weeks. She was confused about why her friends would treat her that way, and she decided to say something to Melissa when she saw her in the hallway.

Zoe suddenly realized that she hadn't been invited to anything for weeks.

"You're always too busy," Melissa protested. "Last month, I invited you to my sleepover, and you couldn't come. Before that, I invited you to the movies, and you were too busy with your mentor's club. You don't seem to have time to spend with any of your friends anymore."

"But we're both on the basketball team," Zoe argued. "I thought maybe we could spend some time together after practice to work on our free throws."

Melissa just shook her head. "Being on the team together is great, Zoe," she said. "But we also need to go out sometimes and just have fun."

"It's true, I've been busy, but as soon as I'm done with the talent contest, we can spend some time together," Zoe promised.

Melissa just rolled her eyes. "That's what you said about the mentor program, and before that, about the holiday toy drive."

Zoe walked away hurt and confused, wondering why her friends didn't seem to understand.

Talk About It

- **Why did Zoe's friends stop hanging out with her?**
- **Do you think your friends should support you in what you do? How should they show their support?**
- **Do you ever feel like your friends aren't supporting you?**

During the basketball semifinals, Zoe couldn't seem to do anything right. Usually, when she felt a little bit tired, she could just concentrate harder and everything would be okay. But this time, she passed the ball wildly, stumbled a few times, and missed the ball when it was passed to her. Zoe's coach took her aside and told her she wasn't in condition to play and probably should sit out for the rest of the game.

"But the team needs me," Zoe said.

"Not like this," the coach replied.

When Zoe got home, she felt dizzy and her knees were shaking. She tried to play a simple tune on her violin, but it was coming out all wrong. She put the violin back and banged the case shut.

"What's wrong?" her mother asked.

Zoe burst into tears as she told her mother how she had been benched at the game and how she was losing her friends. "All I wanted was for you and Dad to be proud of me," she said.

"Of course we're proud of you!" her mother replied.

"But you never say anything about it!" Zoe answered.

Zoe's mom thought for a few moments. "I guess your dad and I are so busy that we forget to let you know it," she finally said. She put down the papers she brought home from work and offered to make Zoe a sandwich.

Zoe was surprised by how hungry she was, and realized that she couldn't remember the last time she'd eaten anything. She finished the sandwich and two glasses of milk and even the leftover spaghetti from the night before. Instead of working on her extra-credit book report, Zoe went to her room to lie down. As she drifted off to sleep, she thought about asking Melissa over on Friday night to eat pizza and watch movies.

Talk About It

- Why do you think Zoe suddenly had trouble at basketball and couldn't play her violin?

- Why is Zoe suddenly so hungry?

- Have you ever worked so hard on something that you forgot to eat or get enough rest? What happened?

Ask Dr. Vicki

Sometimes when people are very driven to do more and more, something else is at work behind the scenes. Zoe might not have realized that she wasn't diving into all those projects to make herself a better person—she was really just trying to get her busy parents to notice her. Often, if she doesn't get the approval she was hoping for, a girl simply tries to reach for something newer, bigger, and more difficult. Suddenly, she might find that she doesn't eat enough, sleep enough, or spend enough time keeping up her friendships. Because she is working at things that seem important, it takes a long time to realize that something is wrong.

Of course, there are always warning signs. In Zoe's case, friends started to complain that they didn't see her much anymore. Then her body and mind stopped performing as well. The more she ignored these signs, the louder they screamed for her attention, until finally, she was too exhausted to do anything.

If you feel that you're turning into a Blur, it's never too late to make a few needed changes. It doesn't mean you should be lazy and do nothing. You simply shouldn't push yourself more than is healthy. Otherwise, one way or another, your body will keep giving you clues until you are forced to slow down and make those changes for your own good.

Get Healthy

1. Pay attention to your body. If you feel that something isn't right inside, get it checked out. Take care of your body by getting enough sleep and eating three healthful meals a day.

2. If you don't have enough time to finish everything you'd like to do, make a list and prioritize the tasks by importance. Then decide which projects will have to wait.

3. If you absolutely, positively must work overtime to finish something, make sure you give yourself a chance to recover afterward.

4. Remember to budget in a little "me" time. This means you should do something simply for enjoyment, not because you expect to get anything else out of it.

The Last Word from MK

The sooner you learn to use your time and energy sensibly, the better equipped you will be for success later in life. Pushing yourself further than you think you can go is okay sometimes, but pay attention to the warning signs. Everyone has limits. The trick is to learn yours and stay within them. When you can do that, you will have the best of all worlds and end up with a happy, healthy, and successful you.

4

The
Pioneer

When you have the right attitude and the determination to finish the job no matter what, you're just about ready to reach for the sky and boldly go where no girl has gone before. To do that, you have to add the last important piece of the puzzle of success: focus. Having focus means keeping your eye on the prize and not being distracted by what others around you are saying or doing. This becomes even more important when you're trying to accomplish something that's never been done before.

Often, you'll feel pressure from those around you to give up on your dream. Some people might even try to convince you that what you're trying to do can't be done or isn't worth doing anyway. They may even call you a dreamer and tell you to get real. But remember, dreamers who knew how to set their mind to a task accomplished the greatest feats in history.

So what's a Pioneer to do? Well, a lot of women who've accomplished unexpected

Dreamers who knew how to set their mind to a task accomplished the greatest feats in history.

things say that it's important to surround yourself with people who believe in you. You also have to be willing to put aside what others want because they don't always understand what's best for you. And that means that while staying focused allows you to achieve your goals, it has another benefit, as well. It's a good way for you to find out who your real friends are!

Fiona was excited about entering a big contest—until her friends made fun of her. But did she let the negativity keep her from going for her goal? Read on to find out.

Fiona's Story

Fiona had her head in the clouds, in a manner of speaking. She was fascinated by anything having to do with flight. She studied all kinds of books and videos about how aircraft fly and even understood things like how the wind moved over a wing to keep a plane in the air. She often made different kinds of paper airplanes to see which one flew the longest and farthest.

One day, she saw a notice on the school bulletin board about a nationwide aircraft design contest for junior high students. The rules were to build an airplane powered by rubber bands. The student whose airplane flew the longest and farthest would win a free trip to Seattle, Washington, to tour the factory where some of the biggest airplanes in the world were made. To Fiona, it was like saying she would be taken to Disneyland.

Fiona thought the airplane design was something she could do really well. But when her friends saw her signing up, they laughed at her. "Who wants to visit a stupid factory?" someone said. Another girl pointed out the list of past winners. None of them came from their school. None were girls. Fiona didn't understand what being a girl had to do with anything or what difference it made that no one in the school had won before. "Well," she said, "I'll just have to be the first."

Talk About It

- **Why do you think Fiona felt so strongly about entering the contest?**

- **Are there some activities that you would like to do, but you think they're not something a lot of girls try?**

- **Have you ever wanted to do something that your friends made fun of? Did you do it? How did you feel?**

Over the next few weeks, Fiona worked busily on her airplane. She had to cut out shapes from balsa wood, which was the lightest wood she could get. She tried out different wing shapes and added fins of different sizes. She experimented with skinny rubber bands and thicker ones, and with different kinds of propellers that she got from model airplane kits. She tried not to think about all the things she was missing—parties, going for ice cream with her family, even her favorite television shows. She knew if she was going to get to the finals, she had to work as hard as she possibly could.

One day, her best friend, Julie, dropped by to see if she wanted to go to the movies.

"I can't," Fiona answered. "I still need to fix my plane so it stays in the air longer. I think I might try using a thicker rubber band. See, it makes the plane heavier but gives it more power."

Julie just snorted. "This is so boring, Fiona. It's a stupid contest. There's so many people trying to win you won't even make it to the finals. You should hang out with me instead."

"Well, it's not boring to me," Fiona answered. "If you had things in your life that were important to you, you would understand why I am working so hard."

"Well, I'm supposed to be your best friend and you don't want to hang out with me, that's what I understand," Julie said. "I guess I'll start hanging out with Tessa from my English class instead. At least she still knows how to have fun."

Fiona didn't know what made her sadder—the fact that she lost Julie as a friend or that Julie never appreciated her love for building airplanes.

Talk About It

- Do you agree with Julie's advice?

- Did Julie want what is best for Fiona or did she have other reasons for talking to her the way she did?

- Have your friends ever tried to talk you out of doing something? What did you do about it?

At school, Fiona noticed that Julie had stopped talking to her. She was worried that she would start losing all her friends. She also felt lonely because no one seemed to believe in her and her project. "Hey, Fee," she heard someone say. "How's the flying going?"

It was Maggie. Fiona would sometimes sit with Maggie at lunch, but she had never really thought of her as a close friend. "Please," Fiona said. "I don't want to hear any more people making fun of me."

"Make fun of you?" Maggie said, shocked. "I'm excited for you! Think of all the girls who want to see a girl win first prize. And think about all of the attention it would bring our school if you won. I mean, it's a national contest. I think what you are doing takes a lot of guts. I hope you win."

When Fiona got home she discovered that her mood was better. She cut a little bit off the tail of the plane and added a fin so it could fly even straighter. She stood at the end of her street, wound the propeller, and got ready to launch her latest model. "This one just might be a winner!" she said and let it fly.

"I think what you are doing takes a lot of guts. I hope you win."

Talk About It

- Why did talking to Maggie make Fiona feel better?

- How do you think the contest turned out? What if Fiona didn't win? Does that mean she shouldn't have tried?

- Have you ever won a competition? Lost? What did it mean to you?

Ask Dr. Vicki

Being a Pioneer means going after something you really believe in and not letting obstacles get in your way. Fiona didn't let the fact that few people believed in her stop her from signing up for the contest. Discovering who you are means exploring possibilities and going after things that feel right for you, not necessarily for other people. If your friends don't support you, then find people who will. At your age, girls are mostly trying to fit in and be accepted; for many of your friends, that means doing what everyone else does. Doing something different may be uncomfortable for your friends, but you need to follow your own dreams, interests, and passions. Go for it—think outside the box—even if your friends want to remain safely inside. What you will find as you follow your own path is that there really is no box, so there are no limits to what you can accomplish.

Get Healthy

1. The most important thing you can do to get through the long struggle toward winning is to picture yourself already there. Holding that in your head can keep you going when things get difficult. Remember that there's always a first time for everything, and records are made to be broken.

2. Don't be surprised when people don't im-mediately support you or even make fun of you. It doesn't mean you have a bad idea or that what you're doing is stupid. It may just mean that some people can't—or won't—try to understand what's important to you.

3. Surround yourself with people who support you. A true friend doesn't try to take you away from your goals; instead, she helps you get there. A little criticism can be help-ful, but if people around you are just plain negative, then find other people who aren't.

4. Your greatest tool is your passion: how strongly you feel about what it is you're trying to accomplish. Trailblazing is not something you do for its own sake. You do it because you feel deep down that this is something that has to be done.

The Last Word from MK

The Pioneer is someone who feels very strongly about what she is doing and has enough confi-dence in her abilities to think she has a chance to succeed. Nothing is certain, and we must all be prepared to face failure, if necessary. But the rewards of blazing a trail far outweigh the risks. So if this is where you think you have the opportunity to really shine, then grit your teeth, make a plan, and focus, focus, focus.

5

The Girl in the Chair

*L*et's face it . . . having any kind of disability is really tough. There are kids who have trouble seeing and kids who have problems hearing, kids who are slow learners and those who have a problem paying attention, kids who stutter when they talk and kids who limp because one leg is shorter than the other. No matter what the disability is, it gets in the way and makes some things more difficult to do. This can be especially challenging at a time when young girls are trying to find their niche within their family, school, or social settings. The added challenge of a disability may be frustrating or overwhelming.

However, there are ways of overcoming or compensating for almost any disability you might have. You may have to work a little harder or use some kind of assistance, but a lot of it has to do with attitude. If you feel sorry for yourself, or see yourself as different and incapable, then you will act that way, and your disability probably will hold you back. But you don't have to let it. You can choose to see yourself as capable in lots of different areas and find a way to go after what you want.

No matter what the disability is, it gets in the way and makes some things more difficult to do.

As Brianna found out, you may have to make some adjustments, but you can still follow the path you want to take. Here's what she did.

Brianna's Story

Ever since fourth grade, Brianna had been "the Girl in the Chair." She had gotten sick back then and because of it, her legs became so weak she could barely use them. When she first had to learn how to use the wheelchair, it took a lot of effort and concentration to get around her school, house, and other places. But now she was very skilled at using the chair, and she got around without even thinking about it. She could do a lot of cool turns and twists and sometimes would show off a little in the hallway.

She also had to adjust to being known as "the Girl in the Chair." But although she was the only one at her school with that kind of disability, Brianna, for the most part, felt as though she was part of normal school life. She had special desks in all her classes that were made wider to fit the wheelchair. She had lots of friends, and she went to parties and dances, where she would rock her wheels and sway along with the music. But Brianna had always liked to compete. Since her illness, she had tried playing games on the Internet and joining the math club and the chess club, but those kinds of competitions didn't hold her interest for very long. She had even tried to play a few sports with other girls—she particularly liked wheelchair tennis—but it was really hard to try to move her chair with one hand and swing her racquet with the other. It was the only thing that made her really sad about her disability. Her friend Becky played on the girls' softball team and often asked Brianna to come watch her games, but Brianna always made up some excuse.

Talk About It

- Do you have a disability? Does it keep you from doing something you really want to do? How do you handle it?

- Is there a "girl in the chair" at your school? How does she adjust? How do the other students treat her?

- Why do you think Brianna never went to any of Becky's softball games?

That year, the girls' softball team made it to the playoffs. It was the final game, and the winning team would be the district champs. Becky was even going to pitch! "You're totally coming, right, Bree?" she asked her.

"Uh . . . I don't know," Brianna said. "You know how I am about sports stuff."

"But this isn't about you," Becky told her. "This is about me—your friend—and it's about your school. We all support you and accept you the way you are. Now how about supporting us the way we are?"

Brianna was a little bit stunned by what Becky said. Nobody had ever spoken to her like that before.

Talk About It

- What do you think of what Becky said to Brianna? What would you have said if you were in Becky's shoes?

- Have you ever had to attend an event to support someone else, even when you didn't want to go? Why didn't you want to go? What happened?

After school let out, most of the kids went to the field to wait for the game to start. As Brianna was leaving, she saw Mr. Wisnicki, the teacher who had taught her chess and suggested she join the chess club. "How have you been, Bree?" he asked warmly. "We don't see you at the club anymore. I guess chess just wasn't exciting enough for you."

"Yeah, sorry," Bree answered. "It was fun to play matches against other students, but I guess I need something that makes me move a little more."

"Have you tried the community center, where you can play sports with other girls with disabilities?" he asked.

"Yes, I go there, too," Brianna answered, "but those are girls I only see when I'm there. I'd like to try competing against the kids I see at school every day."

Brianna wheeled up to the table, took the racket, and concentrated.

"Well, I'm sure you'll find something," he told her. "Don't give up."

The building was almost empty now, but Brianna heard a funny noise coming from the gym. Though she never liked to go in there, she was curious enough to poke her head inside. She saw that someone had put a pair of Ping-Pong tables in a room behind the basketball court. A girl was in there bouncing a ball on the table.

"You want to play?" she asked Brianna.

Brianna wheeled up to the table, took the racket, and concentrated. She wheeled back and forth quickly and handled the racket well, but in the end the other girl beat her by three points. "Hey, you're not bad," she told Brianna. "I'm one of the best players in the school, and you almost beat me."

"I will next time!" Brianna promised.

"Oh, yeah? Wanna play another and we'll see?" she asked. "We can play best out of three."

"Let's do it later," Brianna said, wheeling toward the door. "I think the softball championship game is about to start."

Talk About It

- Why do you think Brianna enjoyed the Ping-Pong game? Do you think it mattered much to her that she didn't win?

- Why did Brianna suddenly decide to attend the softball game?

- Is winning the most important thing to you? Why? Have you ever felt like you've done your best even if you didn't win?

The desire to compete is a natural human drive regardless of any disability you might have. For girls like Brianna who have a strong need to compete, this creates a special challenge. Kids with disabilities have many different options to compete. Competitions such as the Special Olympics and sports such as wheelchair tennis have been created so that people with certain kinds of physical restrictions can play. But Brianna wanted to find some way to compete with her classmates; she didn't want to be put in a separate group. Finding Ping-Pong helped in two ways. She was able to compete in a sport without accommodations. And since she found a sport she enjoyed, watching softball was no longer a painful reminder of what she couldn't do. She then was able to support her friends. Brianna's disability not only made her feel bad about sports in general but also almost interfered with her friendship with Becky. Brianna found something that satisfied her desire to compete, and this made it easier for her to cheer on her friends and her school.

Get Healthy

1. Get out there. Take advantage of the facilities and resources your school and community have to help you be a part of sports teams, or sign up to participate in

other group activities. There are programs and activities to suit every age, skill, and ability.

2. Set a goal. No matter what your limitations are, you can always improve. So give yourself something to shoot for and go for it. Get involved with other kids your age who also are dealing with a disability. Ask your parents, teachers, or doctors about groups and activities geared for people going through the same things as you are.

3. Keep trying. Keep your competitive spirit healthy, and eventually you'll find an area where you can shine.

The Last Word from MK

For girls who are still trying to determine their place in the world, having a disability can make the process even more difficult. But like a lot of life's problems, this one doesn't have one easy answer. Every girl has to find her own individual way of adapting and succeeding. Luckily, the same qualities you'll need—a positive attitude, patience, and determination—are the ones any competitor needs to be the best. And no disability can take those qualities away from you, unless you let it. Your disability doesn't determine your attitude—you do!

6

The Bossy Girl

Okay, so a lot about success may seem as if succeeding depended on you and you alone. But often, the things we're trying to do can't be done alone. You have to get other people to work with you, and that takes leadership.

As a young girl, learning about leadership is extra important. In the adult world, women run corporations, medical centers, and entire countries. When you grow up, you might be one of those women!

A lot of people think leadership just means being the boss. But if that's what you think, then you might be in for a big surprise the first time your leadership is tested. You'll soon discover that there's a whole lot more to it. You have to believe in what you're doing and motivate others to believe in it, too—so that they will work with you to get the job done.

Even if you're the kind of person who finds it easy to tell other people what to do, when you actually do find yourself sitting in the boss's chair, you're bound to make a few mistakes. But don't get discouraged, and don't lose faith in yourself. Before you know it, you'll be comfortably leading the way.

A lot of people think leadership just means being the boss.

Coming from a large family where she was often in charge, Deedee was confident in her leadership abilities. But her classmates didn't end up appreciating her bossy style.

Deedee's Story

For Deedee, telling people what to do seemed like the most natural thing in the world. In her family, she was the oldest of four children, and her parents often left her in charge. If she wanted her little brother to pick up his toy soldiers or her sister to wash the dishes after she used them, she only had to say so, and it was done. After all, if they didn't, there would be trouble once their parents got back!

When her teacher, Ms. Rubenstein, asked who wanted to be the organizer of the school dance, Deedee raised her hand. She didn't think it would be hard at all. But things quickly started to go wrong.

Deedee stood in front of her classmates and announced that the party was going to have a 1980s theme. They would put together music, costumes, and decorations so that the party would seem like it was happening more than twenty years ago.

"Why does it have to be an '80s party?" Crystal asked. "Nobody likes that music."

"I'll tell you why," Deedee answered. "Because I'm in charge of the party, and that's what I say it's going to be."

Talk About It

- Do you think it was a good idea for Deedee to begin by telling her classmates what kind of party they would have?

- Did Deedee answer Crystal's question in a good way, or could she have handled the situation better? If so, how?

- Have you ever been forced to follow someone's idea even though you didn't like it? What did you do?

Deedee told each of her classmates what their job was, but nothing seemed to be happening. She couldn't get any of them to do even the simplest things. She made up a flyer to hang up around the school and asked Dylan to go to the copy room and make a bunch of copies. He refused.

"You *have* to!" she screamed. "I'm in charge of the party."

"So?" he sneered. Deedee found that the louder she shouted, the less things got done.

After a week had gone by, Deedee started worrying that the party was going to be a big failure. She began to think that everybody hated her and that they were purposely trying to make her look bad. She asked Ms. Rubenstein to punish the class for not following her instructions. "That's what my parents would do if this happened at home," Deedee said.

Talk About It

- Was Deedee right when she thought that everyone hated her? If they didn't, why were they not listening to her?

- How else could Deedee have responded to Dylan instead of yelling at him? Has anyone ever shouted at you? How did it feel?

"Deedee, you can't treat the people in class like they are your little brother or sister," Ms. Rubenstein told her. "Just because you were put in charge of this one party doesn't mean you can simply tell everybody what to do and they'll just do it. You have to find a way to work with them so that everybody wants to work hard and make this a great night. Think about how you can get everybody to feel like it's their party, not just yours."

Talk About It

- Have you ever been in charge of your siblings? How is that different from being in charge of a group of your classmates?

- What did Ms. Rubenstein mean when she told Deedee that the class had to feel like it was their party and not just hers?

During a break, Deedee told her classmates that maybe it was time to start over. She asked for suggestions about what would make a great party theme. As people called out ideas, she wrote them on the board. Then Crystal suggested they do "Hip-Hop and Hamburgers."

"I'll bet I can even get my dad to bring the grill and cook the burgers," she said.

"And I can teach some hip-hop moves I've learned at dance class!" said Bethany, sounding excited. Everybody squealed, "Yeah!"

Soon, the entire class started talking about the songs they could bring in, what kind of posters to hang up, and even how many burgers they needed to buy. Suddenly, Deedee realized that she didn't have to give everyone a job or tell anyone what to do. They were so excited that they all volunteered to take on a job they wanted, such as decorating the gym, hanging posters, bringing desserts, and offering to bring their selection

Suddenly, Deedee realized that she didn't have to give everyone a job or tell anyone what to do.

of music. Deedee thought that being a leader was fun when everybody allowed her to lead. She had everyone sign up for the different committees and realized that she just needed someone to take care of wiring the music to the big speakers from the band room. Luckily, Dylan, who had sneered at her before, was being nice to her. He said he knew how things like that worked, and he would take care of it.

Talk About It

- Why did everyone start accepting Deedee as the leader?

- Did the fact that Deedee accepted an idea for the party that wasn't her own make her less of a leader? Why or why not?

- Have you ever been the leader of a group? How did you get the group members to pitch in?

Very often, a girl like Deedee who grew up in a family where she was the boss of her siblings will believe that it's her job to give the orders, and everyone else's job to carry them out. Unfortunately, other people are not likely to accept her authority "just because." And because of this, a Bossy Girl runs the risk of starting out on the wrong foot when dealing with situations outside her own family. She can become confused, angry, and resentful when those around her refuse to follow her lead. Sometimes, out of frustration, she will call people bad names or even threaten them. But guess what? This only makes other people want to work with a Bossy Girl even less!

The trick, as Deedee slowly learned, is to treat other people not as robots, but as who they are: her classmates who wanted to have a say in how their party should be organized. Only by treating others well and getting to know who they are, what they like, and what their special talents are can you get everybody moving in the same direction.

Get Healthy

1. When you find yourself the leader of some kind of team or group, make sure that all the members are united under a common goal.

2. Remember that you are there to help orga-
    nize, not just to give orders. Spend a little time
    getting to know the people you'll be leading.
    Start by asking what they like to do and how
    they think they can best contribute.

3. Be ready to admit mistakes. Just because
    you're in charge doesn't mean you're per-
    fect or that you even have to try to be.

4. Don't think you have to do everything your-
    self or make all the decisions. A good leader
    listens to her group members and allows
    them to take part in decision making.

The Last Word from MK

Good leaders lead. Sometimes that does mean
you have to tell people what to do, but just
as often, you have to hang back and listen.
Occasionally, you might have to put your foot
down, but more frequently, you simply have to
guide people gently. It's a tricky business, and
there's no "playbook" that tells you how to re-
spond to every situation. Like a lot of things in
life, learning how to be a good leader involves
trying your best, making mistakes, and learning from your mistakes so that you can do
even better the next time. So be patient with
yourself—and more importantly, be patient
with others—and you'll all get there together.

7

The Poor Speaker

*L*et's say that you find yourself put in charge of something. You've earned your position because you worked your way up from the bottom. Everybody likes and respects you. Sounds like the perfect recipe for a good leader, don't you think? Well, not so fast.

Sometimes we are put in charge of a project because we've done it many times before and we know how everything is supposed to go. In fact, it all seems so clear to us that we even assume everyone else sees it as clearly as we do. But guess what? Most of the time, it doesn't work that way. For people to understand what you want from them and what it is they're working toward, it is your job to let people know what their task is. And that means learning how to communicate clearly.

Some of us get nervous when we have to talk to a group of people. Others might have trouble communicating in writing. These, too, make it difficult to share ideas and directions. But people have more ways to communicate than ever before. You can call someone using a regular telephone or a cell phone. You can text message. How about an e-mail or an instant message? You can write notes on paper and you can even communicate the old-fashioned way, by speaking face-to-face. With so many ways to get a message across,

With so many ways to get a message across, you can choose which way works best for you, while at the same time strengthening your skills in other areas.

you can choose which way works best for you, while at the same time strengthening your skills in other areas. You'll be surprised at how quickly you become a first-rate, all-around communicator, and you'll have no trouble letting everybody else know it!

Claire had an easy time getting her thoughts down on paper. Unfortunately, she discovered she wasn't so hot a communicator when it came to talking to people face-to-face.

Claire's Story

Claire was the star reporter at her school newspaper, the *Scoop*. Whether it was an article on a recent basketball game or a report on locker break-ins, she always dug deep and found something interesting to say. Claire's articles were so good that even the other "Scoopers," as the paper's staff called themselves, had to try harder just to keep up. Their principal had said that the *Scoop* hadn't been this good in years.

When Claire started seventh grade, her editor, Isabel, had graduated eighth grade, and nobody could think of a better person than Claire to take over the job. Now it would be Claire who would decide which stories would be printed in the *Scoop*. Everyone was looking forward to working with her.

Claire was excited, too, as she went to the first meeting. But when she entered the paper's office, she saw that everybody was sitting in a circle waiting for her to tell them what they were going to be doing.

Claire suddenly felt strange. She wasn't used to this.

Claire suddenly felt strange. As a reporter, her job was to ask other people questions. Now she would have to speak, and they would be the ones asking her questions. She wasn't used to this. "He-hello everybody," she mumbled. "It's good that, you know, we're doing this Scoop, but I want some different, you know . . ."

A few of the Scoopers were looking at each other, and no one was really saying anything.

Talk About It

- Why do you think Claire suddenly found it difficult to speak when she walked into the office?

- Could Claire have done anything before the meeting to make it go better?

- Have you ever found it hard to speak to a group of people even if you've spoken to them lots of times before? Why? What happened?

Claire had big ideas about what the *Scoop* should be like. She dreamed that the *Scoop* would win an award for "Best Junior High School Newspaper." But as the days went by, she noticed that she couldn't get anybody to follow her instructions correctly. For instance, she wanted to do a story about middle school students and their pets, so she sent the paper's photographer, Noah, out to get some pictures. Claire had wanted one picture of the student and one picture of the pet separately, but when Noah brought the pictures in, they were of students walking their dogs, hugging their cats, or holding up a hamster cage.

"Noah, I want to make this like a puzzle, where readers have to figure out which student belongs to which pet," she said irritably. "How can I do that if you have them together in one picture?"

"You didn't tell me that," Noah protested. "You just said, 'Get me some pictures of students and their

pets.' So that's what I did. I didn't know you wanted them in separate shots."

Claire started thinking that the Scoopers just weren't smart enough to understand her new ideas and started doing more and more work herself. Soon, she was running everywhere, trying to finish everyone else's work and do her own, as well.

Talk About It

- Why didn't Claire get the pictures she wanted?

- Do you think it was a good decision for Claire to do all the work herself?

- Have you ever explained something to someone and later found out he or she understood differently? What happened?

One day, Claire's friend Anika, who also worked on the *Scoop*, asked, "Why are you running around all crazy when the rest of us are just waiting for something to do? We're all supposed to be working together. You know, a team?"

"Because nobody will do what I want them to do," Claire answered.

"We can only do that if we understand you, Claire," she replied. "A lot of times you mumble so we can't hear you, or you don't really explain what you mean. It's weird because when we read your articles, you explain everything really well, you know?"

That afternoon, Claire went home and logged on to her computer, preparing to send an e-mail to the Scoopers. She typed a message carefully explaining all the things she had tried to tell the Scoopers when she saw them at school. She read it over and over like she would one of her newspaper stories, changing a few words here and there, adding some new words and taking a few out. Only when she was sure that it said exactly what she wanted it to say did she finally hit Send.

Talk About It

- Why do you think Claire switched to using e-mail to explain herself to the Scoopers?

- In what types of situations do you have the most trouble making yourself understood? How can you improve that?

- Do you think that anything will change at the *Scoop* now that Claire has found a different way to communicate? If so, in what way?

Ask Dr. Vicki

Have you ever seen a television interview with a famous author and realized that even though she writes so well in her books she is actually very shy when she speaks aloud? That's because some people are very good at one type of communication but need help when it comes to another. Luckily, Claire realized this in time so that she was able to get her message across by using written communication, which is how she seems to communicate best.

But girls like Claire still have a ways to go. In order to work as part of a team you need to be able to communicate in as many different ways as possible. So while you can rely on your strong points, you need to work on your other areas at the same time. If you have to give an oral presentation, you can practice it looking in a mirror, in front of a family member, or even by recording it. Like any new skill, the more you practice and the more you use it, the better at it you will become.

Get Healthy

1. Write it down. Written notes make it easier for you to keep track of what you're saying. If you're uncomfortable speaking in front of people, bring very detailed notes. That way, you only have to concentrate on reading them.

2. Speak clearly. Decide what you're going to say, and speak loudly enough so that everyone can hear you. Make sure you're not covering your mouth or turning away before you speak. Looking at your audience gives you an appearance of confidence; the more confidence you seem to have, the more people will listen and take you seriously.

3. Learn to listen. This is the silent half of communication. Regardless of how clear you think your explanations are, take the time to hear back from the people you are communicating with. Otherwise, you'll never really be sure they understand you—or if you understand them!

The Last Word from MK

It's no wonder that so many great leaders in the world are remembered for the beautiful, powerful, or inspiring speeches they gave. After all, clear communication is one of the most important skills a leader must have. But not all of that talent has to be something you were born with. As a matter of fact, since there are so many ways to communicate, it's unlikely that anybody will be good at all of them. And that's why leaders of tomorrow need to work on their communication skills today. Use types of communication you are comfortable with while you work on those that are giving you trouble. As with everything, it just takes practice!

8

The Stand-Up Girl

For many girls, there is nothing scarier and lonelier than being the only one to stand up for something you think is right. Sometimes you can face really intense peer pressure to stay silent and, like everyone else, just go along with whatever is happening. After all, you might even tell yourself, how bad could it be if everyone is doing it?

Well, you know that icky feeling you get inside when you find yourself behaving in some way that you know is wrong just because you don't want to rock the boat? Don't you wish that somebody else would say something, so you wouldn't feel like there's no one standing behind you? Believe it or not, many other people have those feelings, too. And they might all be waiting for just one person to stand up and take the lead, because they are ready to follow. The next time you see something going on that you know is wrong, you don't have to pretend that it's okay.

The next time you see something going on that you know is wrong, you don't have to pretend that it's okay.

Make your feelings known. And sometimes, you'll be as surprised as everyone else is about what happens next!

Kaylee felt like she had to go along with everyone else to fit in, but something about it didn't feel right. Read on to find out whether she ended up doing the right thing.

Kaylee's Story

Kaylee liked gymnastics and had always been good at them. So when she entered junior high, she decided to join the cheerleading squad. She thought it would be fun to cheer the football team on and learn all kinds of new moves. But once she made the squad, she noticed a lot of the girls walked around with an attitude like they were all that.

At lunch, Ashley, the squad captain, would "reserve" a table. It was sort of a rule that all the

cheerleaders had to sit there and that anyone who wasn't a cheerleader could not. Then they would trash all the other girls as they walked by, making fun of them for not being as cool as the cheerleaders were. They singled out one girl, Joanna, who was shy and didn't quite dress like everyone else. Ashley called her Geek-Disease. After she started doing that, no one in the school would sit with Joanna anymore.

Kaylee didn't think that Joanna was such an awful person, and she wouldn't have minded getting to know her better. But Kaylee was a cheerleader now and was afraid to be the only one to go against what all the other cheerleaders were doing. Nearly everyone believed the untrue and sometimes mean things Ashley said about other girls. Kaylee didn't want to be made fun of as Joanna had been.

Talk About It

- Why do you think being a cheerleader made it difficult for Kaylee to get to know Joanna?

- Why did all the cheerleaders listen to Ashley? What do you think would happen if they didn't?

- Have you ever found yourself in a position where everybody was doing something, but you didn't want to go along with it? What did you do?

One day, while waiting outside the school for her mom to pick her up, Kaylee saw Joanna sitting on a bench and reading a book that had a really interesting cover. "What's that about?" Kaylee asked.

"Oh, they're stories about a girl detective who solves crimes that the police can't," Joanna answered.

Just then, Kaylee's mother pulled up to the curb. "I like those kinds of stories too. Maybe we can talk about them more later," Kaylee said, getting in.

"That's what you say now," Joanna replied. "But as soon as the other cheerleaders are around, you'll pretend you don't know me again. That's what everybody does."

Kaylee wanted to tell her it wasn't true, but somehow she just couldn't. She knew that what Joanna said was probably right.

Talk About It

- What are some of the groups at your school? Which group do you fall into? Is that okay with you?

- Have you ever been treated like an outcast? How did you handle it?

- Have you ever treated someone the way the cheerleaders treated Joanna? Why? Did that person really deserve it?

"Who was that girl you were talking to?" Kaylee's mother asked her. "I've never seen her before."

Kaylee explained to her mom that Joanna wasn't the type of girl she usually hung out with, and that's probably why she didn't recognize her. Kaylee told her mom that the cheerleaders hung out with each other

and didn't want to mix with people they considered geeks. That was just how it was. "I don't want it to be like that," Kaylee told her mother, "but it was like that when I first joined the squad. I couldn't make everybody change how they act."

"Well, I don't think you can expect other people to change how they act unless you first change how you act, Kaylee," her mother said. "You need to start

with yourself." That night, Kaylee thought for a long time about what her mom had said. She hoped that she would have the courage to act differently.

The next day, when Kaylee carried her tray from the lunch line, she walked right past the cheerleader table and sat at Joanna's table. Kaylee felt everyone's eyes watching her as she walked past the cheerleaders and knew they were still watching to see what would happen next.

Talk About It

- What did Kaylee's mother mean when she told Kaylee that she needed to start with herself? Do you think that is good advice?

- Why did Kaylee suddenly decide she wasn't going to sit at Ashley's table anymore? Why did she choose to sit with Joanna?

- Have you ever tried to go against what everybody was doing? What did you decide to do? How did it turn out?

All the cheerleaders looked nervously at Ashley to see what she would do. She gave Kaylee a really dirty look and then started to laugh. All the other cheerleaders laughed with her.

Kaylee felt a little awkward and uncomfortable at first, but after she started talking with Joanna she forgot all about Ashley's evil glare. She actually had a lot in common with Joanna. In addition to liking the same types of books, they liked similar music. Soon they were talking like old friends, and even began laughing about Ashley's silly "reserved" table. The lunch period flew right by.

That afternoon at practice, Ashley tried to be extra mean to Kaylee, but Kaylee just ignored her and concentrated on her cheers. Ashley told one of the other cheerleaders to trip Kaylee when she went by, but the girl didn't seem to hear her. When Ashley left, one of the other cheerleaders, Angie, asked Kaylee how she got up the nerve to go sit at another table. Kaylee said, "I just did what I thought was right." She added, "I'm glad I did. Lunch with Joanna was a lot of fun."

The next day at lunch, Angie went over and sat with Kaylee and Joanna. She told Kaylee how happy she was that somebody made it okay to sit at another table. She felt that always hanging around Ashley made it hard to make new friends.

The next Monday, their coach came in to tell them that Ashley unexpectedly had quit the team.

Soon, other cheerleaders began sitting at other tables. No longer did all the cheerleaders sit by each other. In fact, by the end of the week, Ashley was sitting alone.

The next Monday, their coach came in to tell them that Ashley unexpectedly had quit the team, and they needed to elect a new captain. Everyone turned to Kaylee.

Talk About It

- If the other girls had always wanted to sit with other people, why didn't they start doing it until Kaylee did it?

- What would you have done in this situation—be a Stand-Up Girl or wait for someone like Kaylee to make the first move? Why?

- Why did the other cheerleaders want Kaylee to be captain? Have you ever been in charge of a group? What kind of leader were you?

Sometimes in order to fit in, you may find yourself going along with the group and doing something you don't think is quite right. This can create confusion about what you should do. Kaylee didn't want to lose favor with the group, but she thought what they were doing to Joanna was wrong. She thought she would have to convince the entire group that Joanna wasn't so bad before things would change. But like her mother said, when you want to change a situation that's wrong, you don't have to try to change other people's minds. You first have to start with yourself. As long as you listen to your own feelings and behave the way you think you ought to behave, you can change the world around you. It often takes only one person standing up to give others the courage to do the right thing.

Get Healthy

1. Know what's right. Knowing who you are and what you believe in is the best way to prevent being dragged along by others. Make a list of the things you think are important, true, and right, and keep it somewhere where you can see it. Then when you find yourself doing something that goes against what you've written, ask yourself why you are doing it and what you can do to stop it.

2. Your first responsibility is to yourself. Instead of trying to change how other people act, look at your own behavior. Most people don't want to be the first one to be different. It takes a leader to make the first move. When you do, it's like giving other people permission to do the same thing.

3. Expect resistance. When people have fallen into a pattern of behavior and you suddenly decide to act differently, those around you may act badly and even lash out. This is the time for you to be your strongest.

The Last Word from MK

Often when people are simply following the leader and doing things that they know deep down are wrong, they are secretly waiting for someone to come along and show them that it's okay to stand up and do the right thing. Remember, Kaylee succeeded not by trying to change the cheerleaders—or the school in general—but by listening to her own inner voice that told her right from wrong and then changing her own behavior. It doesn't take a big effort. All you have to do is stand up and do what you believe is right for you.

9

The Pushover

For many adolescent girls, it's hard to resist the desire to be popular. We seem to really want other people to like us so we feel special. And because of that strong desire, it's easy to fall into the trap of doing things just so other people will be our friends.

This becomes even trickier when we talk about leadership. Yes, leaders have to be popular. Otherwise, who would vote for them? But to be a really good leader, you can't just do what other people want because you're afraid that they won't like you if you don't. You have to do what's best for the group you are leading. How do you do that? Well, many women in leadership positions would tell you that you first have to like yourself and believe in what you're doing. Then, you become a person who people want to like and follow. Just ask Julie, who would do almost anything to get people to like her.

Julie's Story

For much of Julie's life, whenever anyone asked her what she wanted to be, only one thing came to mind: she wanted to be popular. Julie often imagined herself one day being famous and admired. All that mattered was for everyone to love her and to want to be her friend.

At school, she worried a lot about whether she would be invited to all the parties and if lots of people would show up to hers. Sometimes, she gave away her favorite dessert that her mom packed with her lunch, or helped girls write their papers just so they'd be her friends. The problem was that a lot of the other kids realized this about Julie. While Julie thought she was one of the popular girls in school, behind her back, people started calling her the Pushover.

Julie often imagined herself one day being famous and admired. All that mattered was for everyone to love her and to want to be her friend.

One day, Julie asked her homeroom teacher, Mrs. Ikeda, if she could lead the junior high's Save Our Planet Committee. The committee would be part of a nationwide program in which students figured out ways their school could save energy, pollute less, and help make the earth a greener, better place.

"It's a big responsibility, Julie," Mrs. Ikeda told her. "Are you sure you can handle it?"

"Sure," Julie said. She knew she would be able to handle it, especially since she was interested in the environment. However, she was mainly thinking that leading the committee was a good way to become even more popular.

Talk About It

- What do you think about Julie's reasons for wanting to lead the Save Our Planet Committee?

- Do you ever do things for other people so they will like you? Is that a good reason?

- Have you ever pretended to like someone just so they'd do you a favor? What happened?

Leading the committee meant Julie needed to organize a lot of tasks. Some of them were fun and others not so fun. For instance, someone had to make a cool sign for the parking lot to tell parents to turn off their engines when they were waiting to pick up their kids. But who wanted to put on big rubber gloves and inspect the garbage to see if the school was really doing its best at recycling?

Paula, one of the girls on the committee, told Julie she would love to paint the sign. Julie had first thought that Amanda should do it, because everyone knew that Amanda was the best artist in the class. "So, you don't believe I can do as good a job as Amanda?" Paula said. "Well, some friend you are." Julie squirmed a little and then said, "Okay, sure, you can paint it."

That made Paula happy, and everything was okay until Julie ran into Amanda.

"How could you do that?" Amanda cried. "Paula's not even an artist!"

Julie didn't want to lose Amanda's friendship either, so she said, "Well, I guess you should do the sign."

"So now we're going to have two signs?" Amanda asked. "There's only one signpost." Amanda turned and walked away in annoyance. Julie knew both girls would be mad at her. She had no idea what she was going to do about that or the committee.

Talk About It

- Who do you think should paint the sign? Why?

- Have you ever had to make a choice that you thought was best, even if it affected a friendship? How did it turn out?

Two weeks later, Mrs. Ikeda asked Julie how the committee was going, but Julie had to admit she hadn't gotten very far. She had told too many people they could do fun things. Nobody would want to do the hard things, and some of them were very important for the committee's success. "I'm so afraid that people will hate me if I don't let them do what they want to do, but now everybody is angry with me anyway," Julie said.

"Julie, if you treat the Save Our Planet Committee like it's a popularity contest, you're not going to be popular or help save the planet," Mrs. Ikeda told her.

Mrs. Ikeda suggested that first Julie should try to better understand what the committee was about and then decide what to do. Julie watched some videos and researched global warming on the Web. She also started really paying attention to things at the school that could be changed to save energy or create less garbage. Julie realized that being involved on the committee was a perfect

"Julie, if you treat the Save Our Planet Committee like it's a popularity contest, you're not going to be popular or help save the planet," Mrs. Ikeda told her.

way for her to start paying more attention to what she wanted and what made her happy, which included the environment. Julie made her decision on what to do with Paula and Amanda.

When Julie saw Paula at the next meeting, she talked to her about the committee's needs. Julie told Paula that Amanda's artistic ability could be best put to work by her making the sign. Amanda was best for that particular assignment, and that meant that it was best for the committee. Julie also explained to Paula that she realized the school's trash problem was so big it was going to take two people to check whether students were really recycling like they were supposed to. "So I'll be helping you," she said.

"You will?" Paula asked.

"Sure," said Julie. "After all, what are friends for? I even got rubber gloves and face masks for protection. Come on. You won't have to touch or smell anything."

Paula still seemed a little unsure, but she agreed.

Even though the garbage bags were full of all kinds of gross things, the girls were soon giggling over all the weird stuff they found and making jokes about how silly each of them looked in their rubber gloves and face masks. The work seemed to go quickly, and after they were finished, Paula invited Julie to come over to her house to wash up and have dinner.

Talk About It

- What lesson did Julie learn? How did that help her be a good leader?

- What do you think of Julie's decision? What would you have done in her position?

- Would you like to be a leader? What kinds of opportunities does your school have?

Julie really had two lessons to learn: One is that it doesn't pay to try to make people like you. In fact, being a Pushover means that people actually respect you even less than if you just let them decide if they like you based on who you really are. Julie also learned that it's not enough for a leader just to be popular, but that a leader also has to command respect. And nobody gets more respect than people who are committed to what they believe in.

By offering to help Paula go through the trash, Julie showed that being the leader didn't make her better than anyone else, and that she wasn't asking Paula to do something she wasn't willing to do herself. After that, she didn't have to worry about Paula liking her. Their friendship was able to happen on its own. Paula ended up liking Julie for who she was, not because she had done something nice for her.

Friendship involves lots of give and take. If you find that you are doing all the giving and the other person is doing all the taking, then you have found a user, not a friend. Stay away from people who like you only for what you can do for them. Look for people who like you for being yourself; they are the ones who can become your true friends.

Get Healthy

1. Make friends with yourself first. Think about what you like about yourself. You might even want to make a list of all your likeable qualities.

2. Make decisions that are right for you. If someone threatens that you need to give into her demands or she won't be your friend, she already isn't. True friends don't use the relationship as a bargaining tool.

3. Be a true leader. Taking on a leadership role means doing what's best for the goal of the group, not what's best for you personally.

The Last Word from MK

The pushovers of the world get so caught up in whether or not they're going to be popular that they forget about what is really important to them. The funny thing is, when you act like you want everyone to be your friend, you don't really make any true friends. Worse still, it's hard to get people to follow your lead. It's only when you like yourself enough to use your leadership position to truly accomplish something more than popularity, you will find yourself surrounded by real friends and people who can help you reach your goals.

A Second Look

One thing I really hope that you get from all of these stories is that you are not alone. The problems you're facing and the feelings you're having are things that many girls your age are going through. Not only that, but many adult women—yes, even the people you look up to and follow—went through the very same struggles when they were young.

I also hope you take this from these stories: no matter who you are or what the circumstances may be, you can choose to accept them or work to make them better. When finding yourself in these positions, the key is having the right attitude and mind-set to push you through the situation and on toward success. It's really about persistence and learning from your mistakes. These two things are vital for success at any age.

What makes you more fortunate than anyone before you is that you now have their examples to learn from. It doesn't matter if you've never succeeded at anything in your life or if you've never been in charge before. At one time or another, everybody was in that very same position. But those who have learned to change their attitude, sharpen their focus, and stick with it no matter what have not only reached some amazing goals, but they've often also succeeded in getting other people to follow them. I should know. I was one of those people. And I hope you can follow, at least a little bit, in my footsteps. Because if you do, then I will have succeeded, and so will you!

XOXO,
MK

Pay It Forward

Remember, a healthful life is about balance. Now that you know how to walk that path, pay it forward to a friend or even to yourself! Remember the Get Healthy tips throughout this book, and then take these steps to get healthy and get going.

- Spend time thinking about what you are passionate about. Know who you are and what you believe in. This is the best way to guard against being pulled along with the crowd or being pressured into something you don't want to do!

- Take time to think about what you would like to accomplish in the future. What are your interests and skills? What do you get excited about?

- Set smaller goals to help you reach these accomplishments, even if they are things you would like to achieve years in the future. Set yourself up for success by taking active steps today to put yourself in line with where you want to be when you grow up.

- If you need to, set up little rewards for yourself every time you achieve a goal. For example, you can download that new song, but only after you've reached your goal.

- Make lists. This is a great way to monitor your progress and keep yourself on track. Seeing all of the things you have achieved and crossed off your list is also a great way to stay motivated!

- If you get discouraged, use your imagination and picture yourself reaching your goals. This can give you the encouragement you need to keep pushing forward.

- Be social. Get to know all kinds of people, some who are like you and some who are different from you. Practice your listening and communication skills as you make new friends and spend time with your family.

- When you find yourself leading a team or a group, make sure that all of the members are united under a common goal. Take the time to get everyone on the same page before you begin working. This way, your teammates will respect you, because you've shown that you respect them.

- As a leader, make decisions that are best for the group and its overall goals. You will actually gain a lot more personal benefit from being the strong leader you are capable of being.

Additional Resources

Select Bibliography

Deak, Joan. *Girls Will Be Girls: Raising Confident and Courageous Daughters*. New York: Hyperion, 2003.

Doyle, Mary K. *Mentoring Heroes: 52 Fabulous Women's Paths to Success and the Mentors Who Empowered Them*. Batavia, IL: 3E Press, 2000.

Hartley-Brewer, Elizabeth. *Raising Confident Girls: 100 Tips for Parents and Teachers*. Cambridge, MA: Da Capo Press, 2001.

Mackoff, Barbara. *Growing a Girl: Seven Strategies for Raising a Strong, Spirited Daughter*. New York: Dell Publishing, 1996.

Further Reading

Bachel, Beverly K. *What Do You Really Want? How to Set a Goal and Go for It! A Guide for Teens*. Minneapolis: Free Spirit Publishing, 2001.

Covey, Sean. *The 7 Habits of Highly Effective Teens*. New York: Fireside, 1998.

Devillers, Julia. *GirlWise: How to Be Confident, Capable, Cool, and in Control*. New York: Three Rivers Press, 2002.

Rimm, Sylvia B. *See Jane Win for Girls: A Smart Girl's Guide to Success*. Minneapolis: Free Spirit Publishing, 2003.

Web Sites

To learn more about success and leadership, visit ABDO Publishing Company on the World Wide Web at **www.abdopublishing.com**. Web sites about success and leadership are featured on our Book Links page. These links are routinely monitored and updated to provide the most current information available.

For More Information

For more information on this subject, contact or visit the following organizations.

Girlstart

1400 West Anderson Lane, Austin, TX 78757
512-916-4775
www.girlstart.org
Girlstart, an organization focused on motivating girls to excel in math and science, hosts camps and seminars to give hands-on experience for girls wanting to explore these fields.

New Moon

2 W First Street, #101, Duluth, MN 55802
800-381-4743 or 218-728-5507
www.newmoongirlmedia.com
This advertisement-free publication for girls seeks to encourage girls to speak up and be heard.

Glossary

criticize
To review, analyze, or evaluate the quality of something.

determination
Being fixed on a goal or end result and consistently moving toward it.

disability
A physical or mental restriction that makes it more difficult for a person to do certain things.

focus
To concentrate on one thing.

global warming
An increase in Earth's atmospheric temperature resulting in climate changes.

mentor
A trusted friend or family member who counsels, gives advice, or provides encouragement.

motivate
To encourage someone.

obsession
An idea or a thought that a person cannot stop focusing on and is continually preoccupied with.

outcast
Someone who is not accepted by other people.

prioritize
To arrange things in order of importance or urgency.

sacrifice
To give up something important or enjoyable for a good reason.

Special Olympics
Games and sports for those with mental or physical disabilities.

Index

About the Author

MK Ehrman is a freelance writer with a degree in psychology who's written on a variety of topics for such newspapers and magazines as the *Los Angeles Times, Teen People, Sunset, Nickelodeon,* and many others.

Photo Credits

Yukmin/Getty Images, 12; Izabela Habur/iStock Photo, 17; Image Source/AP Images, 22, 37, 43, 45, 62; Ned Frisk/Getty Images, 27; Inti St. Clair/Getty Images, 35; Tim Jones/Getty Images, 47; Alistair Scott/iStock Photo, 52; Bonnie Schupp/iStock Photo, 57; SW Productions/ Jupiterimages/AP Images, 64; Chris Schmidt/iStock Photo, 67; Thomas Barwick/Getty Images, 74; iStock Photo, 77; Michelle Malven/iStock Photo, 82; Jim Pruitt/ iStock Images, 85; Baerbel Schmidt/Getty Images, 86; Zia Soleil/Getty Images, 89; Jacom Stephens/iStock Photo, 96; ColorBlind Images/Getty Images, 99